Into Eros
Zoe Brigley

VERVE
POETRY PRESS
BIRMINGHAM

PUBLISHED BY VERVE POETRY PRESS
https://vervepoetrypress.com
mail@vervepoetrypress.com

All rights reserved
© 2021 Zoe Brigley

The right of Zoe Brigley to be identified as author of this work has been asserted in accordance with section 77 of the Copyright, Designs and Patents Act 1988.

No part of this work may be reproduced, stored or transmitted in any form or by any means, graphic, electronic, recorded or mechanical, without the prior written permission of the publisher.

FIRST PUBLISHED OCT 2021

Printed and bound in the UK
by Positive Print, Birmingham

ISBN: 978-1-912565-67-2

Cover Artwork: *Learning the Last Bright Routes*
by Victoria Brookland

CONTENTS

The Pumpkin Flowers Take Pleasure Too	6
It Might Be Impossible for Her to Love	7
When I Touch the Poison Sumac, I Become it Too	8
She Tells You About the Second Time	10
Antoinette Cento	11
What They Say About Antoinette	12
Bloom Sonnets	13
Frog Town	15
Somehow Despite Everything	16
The Last Days of August	17
The Apple Blossom Persuades the Bee	18
You Loved Her Body	20
Circle Poem	21
Monarch	23
The Moon Laughs Over Quarantine	24
Still She Survived	25
Imprint	26
At Magdala	27
Psych- : An Erasure After John Keats	28
She Has Found Her Own Pleasure	31
Erotica for the Print Makers	32
After the Yanartaş	33

Your story begins the moment Eros enters you. That incursion is the biggest risk of your life.
—Anne Carson

Love is awful. It's painful. Frightening. It makes you doubt yourself, judge yourself, distance yourself. It takes strength to know what's right. And love isn't something that weak people do.
—*Fleabag*

Into Eros

The Pumpkin Flowers Take Pleasure Too

At dawn, pumpkin flowers loosen themselves
for the rain. Male buds in bloom for weeks give
way to females flowering. Incandescent,
vivid orange, petals open: submissive
like a wild creature folding back its ears:
the stigma like a nipple. But a teacher
once told me that humans are *"the only
species that evolved to make sex a pleasure
for females."* Still the pumpkin flowers stand
engorged without shame or fear & what feeling
when the bee completes its dusty circuit,
brush of fur from its tight, hard body? Now
flowers are shutting slowly, delicately: a woman
crossing her legs: lips closing after a kiss.

It Might Be Impossible For Her To Love

the way she wants to because sometimes at night
or even during the day
she is afraid   just a regular hike
through the woods, along the railroad track

she is walking there
when a sound   a liquid sound
of hinges creaking   just a branch in the wind
just a hand on the door   but who is there
who is stepping through?   is this memory?
is this what you do   in the aftermath?

When I Touch Poison Sumac, I Become It Too

I wish I could tell which ones are sumac, like
the time me & M went back to that actor's

house & because I was tired, I lay down on
the bed, where he put one leg over me, pinned

my arms to the pillow: my *No* stung, stopped
him like poison sumac's chemistry of self-

defence. Or maybe the sumac was him, because
once poison sumac touches the skin it can't

be removed with soap & water. But now I am
running into the field where the swifts are flying,

their movements sharp & close to the ground. I did
what they asked. I took the pain into myself:

that's how sumac works, chemicals
binding with cells, so the body attacks

itself, no longer knows its own skin cells:
immunity working to fix, trim, make me

palatable. When I run in the woods
I pretend I'm not afraid. But I don't

always recognize poison sumac when it grows
& soon the tap root extends so deep I can't

dig it out. I tape up my knees & shoulders
so I am fixed perfectly. My stomach jolts

because the creak of a twisting branch in the wind
sounds like a door opening: a human thing

unwelcome in the wild. I used to think
the shushing leaves were talking to me, but trees

only speak under the earth & only to
each other. It was the wind if anything

that day, sweeping the canopy with despair:
leave him, run, leave, run. I did leave the city

where each night under my window a drunk would sing
& the glass rattled as though hands had shaken it.

I moved deep into the country: still smarting.
But there's something else I'm running towards:

it's you dragging me back into my body: you
I want to touch me: hot wind blowing

where skins of leaves rub together
with a whispery sound. But sumac berries

swell & tease the mouth like a thought, or
maybe just hormones warm on the air

with a little tinge of death just like fucking.

She Tells You About The Second Time

with that other man when he told her he
was dumping her   she tells how
walking home from the bar he said
the words   and her legs   collapsed he carried her
back to the house   took off
her clothes while she cried   she asks *what kind
of a person then decides they want to violently
fuck you?*   sometimes she reminds herself
you are not him   though you are a man *of course*
she says *he didn't actually break up with me*

Antoinette Cento

You can pretend for a long time but one day
it all falls away and you are alone: always
two deaths: the real one, and the one people
know about. I must remember chandeliers
and dancing: ladders and roses and snow: the yellow
handkerchief I wore round my head tied
at the front in Martinique fashion. He hates me
and I hate him. We'll see who hates best. Unhappily
children do hurt flies. Have all beautiful things sad
destinies? I wrote it down several times, and
always it looked like a damn cold lie to me.
The dress on the floor: fire spread across
the room. Does it make me look intemperate
and unchaste? They say when trouble comes, close
ranks: rich white people always do. On the battlements
it was cool and I could hardly hear them. It was
wrapped in a leaf, what she had given me, and
I felt it smooth and shiny, against my skin.

What They Say About Antoinette

Women's madness is an intelligible response to unlivable conditions in which other modes of response are blocked off.
—Janet Wirth-Cauchon

He says there is a strange,
uncomfortable feeling to her. Like a dream
of someone speaking
in a language from a different
century. Like another
species. Each moment with her is too
strained, too full, and too empty. She is afraid
of being abandoned, because long ago
she abandoned herself. She lives
on the fringes of things: princess,
witch, trickster, but
fairy tale figures usually turn to flesh. They say
that if the hysteric is damaged, the borderline
woman is worse, but still you are left
guilty for ever believing
she was anything
other than
genuine.

Bloom Sonnets

I thought well as well him as another and then I asked him with my eyes to ask again yes and then he asked me would I yes to say yes
        —Molly Bloom

It happens in the room where she paints her
self. Ice falls. A few light taps. Is it snow
that makes the noise on the windowpane? But
no, a high pitch: more like the whine
of a piano tuner's fork. A man
came in, said she had a good voice. *If you
said yes once, then why ask again?*
was what he told her when the business
was done, but he knew it was wrong: how yes
can mean no when said with tears, a frown. *I think
they have an OK time just because...* But
she asks: *How do you know?* Like Meg Ryan
who failed to be convincing enough, so
the director showed her how. Yes. Yes. Yes.

Yes, I grow to hate snow. Here, it's something
to dig a way out of: the spade scraping
stacked concrete: flakes too thin to even
roll to a ball. I am pressing my cheek
up against the frost. Even the bones are
cold and purplish, gray as ostrich feathers.
But here is my eye on the sharp white shapes
that ice crystals make, on how much you can see
up close if you look. *Yes yes I will yes...*
On honeymoon in Tarifa: Atlas
Mountains across the strait: legs in the sand:
so many nights asleep: roses blowing: bridegroom
taking photographs: *I will wear a red*
yes, and how he kissed me yes I will yes

Frog Town

An afternoon hunkering under late July heat
& frogs are speaking: their songs all scratch,
squelch, elastic plunk. Sun-basking frogs
turn their burnished wet skins under sun, or
frog-bodies splash, slather & slap the ancient
water of the pond. *But why does the long grass
tremble & quake as if it had been touched?*

As for me, a hundred tiny stings on
a pale expanse of bare legs: proboscides
tickling, sucking. Later, from the airport
I burst with laughter at 10,000 feet, high
over frog-town, its lives small under
the shadow of a wing: irresistible
engines: the jet roaring, howling.

Somehow Despite Everything

Eros still strikes her in cycles in changing seasons
in the lush   hot wind that flusters
the flat land where she lives some nights
she dozes on the patio a slight breeze moving
among the trees in her hair across closed eyelids
her skin a seismometer to the sensuous
she has learned not   to regard herself but look
out there where one morning under a squall
the pumpkin flowers open up to the rain

The Last Days of August

After James Tate

Through gaps & crannies in
the clapboard house blows the hot wind
to quicken a ghost of a lover

& me. All day it has travelled over
the plains & now it trembles across
my cheap drapes. Is it the wind or

a lover from faraway? Like the cold
breeze that tapped on my grandmother's
door the night Grandpa died & every night

after: the knocking. There it is again but
warm as breath, singing the blast
of the train whistle & I am nothing

if not hungry. For it is the end of August, &
I know—love is hitched to the tracks, blown
through, travelling away across America.

The Apple Blossom Persuades the Bee

A hum whirring, shushing, and
sh-zip
when a wing in motion hits a leaf. Who is that
moving, easy on the hot wind? But

before you pass
again, you must
listen: I am close
to death.

Around me, tiny legs
are dragging sticky along a leaf,
a moan,
the breeze in the branches.

Pink
and bare
in my longing, do I
not tempt you?

So quickly it is
over: a brief
tumescence, then dry
branches rasping over

and over. My desire reaches
down swollen through wood, down
into the strings of the earth
that pull and suck

gently. I am beside myself: pollen
on the breeze quickening. After the first love,
there will be
no other.

You Loved Her Body

but could not fathom her aftermath tremors even now
inside her a sharp   voice repeating *it's my*
fault it's my fault   *it's me it's me* though if
you'd thought   about it you'd know
it wasn't true   but you couldn't   face it caught
as you were   by your own fear

Circle Poem

I also live alone, though
I exist among many,

grind sequins with mortar &

stone, have eaten earth from a yogurt pot.

There are possums in the garden that come carrying
       the moon in their paws,
dropping it in the lake, where on occasion we might
       see an egret,
       still & white & shaped
like a microphone stand. It leans dipping its beak like
       a knife-blade into
       the circle of water long after moonrise. I live

in a boomtown, where all the time they are shifting

blocks around, never clear where I stand, but
       I flag down cars with the flag of my dress, while
              passers-by shout: *That looks great on you.* I am loose

here: not loose like a dress spun & stretched
       on high heat, but loose like a silver earring when
the clasp won't quite close & one day it falls in the grass
              somewhere. I have lived in
cookie cutters, shiny as chrome on a 1942 Pontiac streamliner;
       lived in
       the small white berry

                   of poison sumac; or in the closed
                          anemone exposed out of water, angry in its sac. I am forced
into wire & cables, where
          there exists a solar system but not like our own,
our sun unique,
                   because it is alone without companions.
          More common

                   in the night sky are
          two or more stars that orbit each
other, you & I held together by gravity. I live in a telescope
                   pointing up, where
          some pairs are so close they start
to become one: the spiral disk of the white dwarf reels
in a red giant
          & blasts between them brilliant light.

Monarch

How sensuous her forest walk: logs split
in the dark glade, or lying helpless where
they fall: leaves shivering as though fingers
had grasped them: the humming of insects or
wires. You are the last monarch of summer, king
on your huge red wings. She cannot catch you
to tell if you are handsome or not, but
there's a largeness of spirit she cannot
deny. Which is to say that she wishes you
would light upon her, or arrive in the form
she loves best: become a black swallowtail
with blue on its wings. She hardly feels you
land, attracted by sweetness: sweat or lotion.
Here, you can do it. You show her how—

The Moon Laughs Over Quarantine

First there was silence the way / a room fills with absence:
    a lag, lack, scratchiness / of need. Perhaps we were

voided before we began, but / when I make myself hard
    and glittering I think / you are half in love with me.

Maybe this is all there is, all / there can be but see how
    I conjure blossoms suspended / mid-air, or perhaps

they are tiny flakes of snow on / the breeze? Touch them. See
    if they are cold. Early / morning pre-dawn, and

the pink moon is laughing / over quarantine. I tried
    all night to pray to / a plaster figure of Mary, but

the moon bends in through / my curtains, and in sleep, a hawk
    tells me: *She will never / come to you now*. No blessing.

When I was born my ears were / pointed like an elf's, and
    there's a mark: a strawberry at / the base of my spine

from that time when I fell / down the stairs. I am so tired
    of conjuring your love out / of the air. Tonight, I'll put

on my sea-green silks and / drive out into the lockdown
    to the lakeshore with an open / gate where I wade in

murky water. Don't ask the moon. / She'll tell you the more
    you love someone the less / they love you back.

Still She Survived

    and there was   something left
    behind that kept her   alive   the girl she was
        before all this
                        she's
    still here the girl   who daydreamed
    about Eros, felt   it
    run through   her electricity or blood

Imprint

Darling, I'll never know what love is for, until the night
I undress before you. I'll wear nothing but

my bronze hair & the prettiest ribbons. When the drapes
fall down I'll be gold in the firelight, luminous

the skin. What if I said that I dreamed you (if
you ever existed)? Imprint, imago behind

my eye: a man, strong & gentle enough to hold a wild
creature like me: vixen, sharp-toothed & sniffing

the air. I would give myself up to your voice if you tell me:
be still. When you put your hands on me, I am still.

At Magdala

*They said to her, "Woman, why are you weeping?" She
said to them, "They have taken away my Lord, and I do
not know where they have laid him."*
    —John 20.13

My lover comes to me in Galilee, white
dress wet and stuck to my skin, and his hands
are reaching, the lake surface refracts,
ripples: a mouth that sucks us. A cold shock
of water against the skin can kick start
the heart to leaping. I measure how I grow

against his shoulder, how on tiptoes I can
stretch my arms about his neck. Or sometimes
I am low with myrrh and oil: his foot
cradled, slippery hands, lips, fingers deep
in arches. There is no humiliation
for I am a cedar casting a woody

sweetness on the air, but always alone, stood
in the high place of my humility. For what will I
be forgiven? What can I give but my hands,
the quickness of a turning mind, a candle
carried like love over the dark water?

Psych-: An Erasure After John Keats

        hear   tuneless numbers
        sweet   and   dear
                                            secrets should be sung
                                      soft-conched
I dreamt   did I see
                                                    eyes
                in a forest
                          fainting
                creatures
            deepest   whispering
   leaves   trembled blossoms
                            scarce

            cool-rooted flowers
    blue, silver-white, and budded
                calm-breathing   bedded
  their arms
  their lips
     disjoined
      ready   kisses
                    dawn
                    winged
but who   O
     his

      latest born   loveliest

fairer   star

```
         vesper          glow-worm
                                temple
                         heaped with
                                        delicious moan
                                  midnight
                                         incense
                  chain-swung
                                  oracle   heat
                                           prophet



           brightest
                     too late
           holy                   haunted
                                  and the fire
                         these days
                                           lucent
         fluttering
    I see and sing
                                           make a moan
                upon the midnight
                voice
                                           teeming
                heat
                of pale-mouth     dreaming



    yes I will be
                     untrodden
                branched            new grown
                         pines   murmur
                                           dark-cluster'd
```

29

      fledge

                        streams, and birds, and bees,
          moss-lain   lulled
          in the midst of this
                will I dress
with   a working brain
             buds and bells and stars
                  gardener
         breeding flowers
                          all soft
           shadowy
               a casement
                   love

She Has Found Her Own Pleasure

and will again but   still the balance between
the loving she needs   and the risk
of Eros sweet   bitter but who can resist
the gorgeousness of   the world the pull
of   the heart the sensuous   nature of things?

Erotica for the Print Makers

If you could press her look onto paper, it would be
bliss, an expression fixed by eyelids that close
on pleasure, the shivering lashes, what colors

the eyes see behind their lids. You would draw
a mouth making an O of delight, the lips so heavy, swollen
with kisses, like a sudden rush of blood, & him too—

you would print his ecstasy in a chin tilting up,
the neck arching with the little movements of the head,
which turns as if looking for something, though again

the eyes are closed. You could notice the arching
of her feet, the curling and uncurling of the toes, or how
her lover's chest expands with a great intake of breath.

You would sketch her hair as a storm of gold raining
upon his face & show their coupling for what it is: the ripe
complication of two bodies. You would reproduce

carefully the tiny hairs erect on the lovers' bodies & how
as the lovers slide together, they reach for one another
with their mouths, with their hands, with their skins.

After the Yanartaş

Yes, you have changed me. Now
I shiver like flaming Yanartaş: out
of the dry bedrock I dance, a hundred
tiny fires, such power in smallness.

                        Tell them

do not underestimate me. Wherever rock
is opened by frost or blow, I come
snaking out, sharp in my nakedness.
I would not hurt you, would not

contain you, though what you
have felt until now is only a half
heat, what you have seen until now
is only a veil over smoke. You will

know me when you find me, golden
in the dawn, shearing the roses
with such deft grace. I have waited
so long my hair hangs

to my waist, but I pressed
your memory between the pages
of a Greek history tome. It is blue
as ever, though fragile as moth wings.

When I see you again, I will place
the dry leaves on your tongue where
they will melt to singed sugar, and
all I'll be saying is: Remember.

ACKNOWLEDGEMENTS

Jean Rhys is drawn on in 'Antoinette Cento', which is a found poem from lines in Rhys's *The Wide Sargasso Sea*. 'What They Say About Antoinette' is a found poem made of testimonies in Janet Wirth-Cauchon's study *Women and Borderline Personality Disorder*. Jean Rhys was posthumously diagnosed with Borderline Personality Disorder.

'The Last Days of August' was inspired by James Tate's poem 'The Last Days of April. 'Bloom Sonnets' refers to James Joyce's *Ulysses,* and was inspired by Frank Shovlin's essay 'Who Was Father Conroy? James Joyce, William Rooney, and "The Priest of Adergool", from *James Joyce Quarterly* 47.2. 'Psych-' is an erasure of John Keats' 'Ode to Psyche.' 'Imprint' was inspired by the first line of a poem by Leanne O'Sullivan's poem 'Valentine' : 'Darling, sometimes I know what love / is for.'

Poems from this manuscript have been published in the U.S. in *Feminist Formations* and *Gulf Coast* and in the UK in *Bad Lilies* and *Unfinished Creatures.*

Thank you to the friends who read drafts of these poems, especially Adrian Matejka, Kristian Evans, Carrie Etter, Aaron Kent, Hannah Lowe, Sue Mackrell, Fleming Meeks, and the circle of Welsh women poets: Emily Cotterill, Rhian Edwards, Julie Griffiths, Mab Jones, and Susie Wildsmith – remember that wonderful summer in Wales when we stayed up into the night reading each other's poems!

Thanks, above all, to those who fight to undo the inequalities in our intimacies with others. How natural and invisible these strictures seem, and how hard it can be to forge a relationship based on equality and mutual respect, but there is the possibility of freedom. May we all find that freedom. I wish it for you.

ABOUT VERVE POETRY PRESS

Verve Poetry Press is a quite new and already award-winning press that focussed initially on meeting a local need in Birmingham - a need for the vibrant poetry scene here in Brum to find a way to present itself to the poetry world via publication. Co-founded by Stuart Bartholomew and Amerah Saleh, it now publishes poets from all corners of the UK and beyond - poets that speak to the city's varied and energetic qualities and will contribute to its many poetic stories.

Added to this is a colourful pamphlet series, many featuring poets who have performed at our sister festival - and a poetry show series which captures the magic of longer poetry performance pieces by festival alumni such as Polarbear, Matt Abbott and Genevieve Carver.

The press has been voted Most Innovative Publisher at the Saboteur Awards, and has won the Publisher's Award for Poetry Pamphlets at the Michael Marks Awards.

Like the festival, we strive to think about poetry in inclusive ways and embrace the multiplicity of approaches towards this glorious art.

https://vervepoetrypress.com
@VervePoetryPres
mail@vervepoetrypress.com